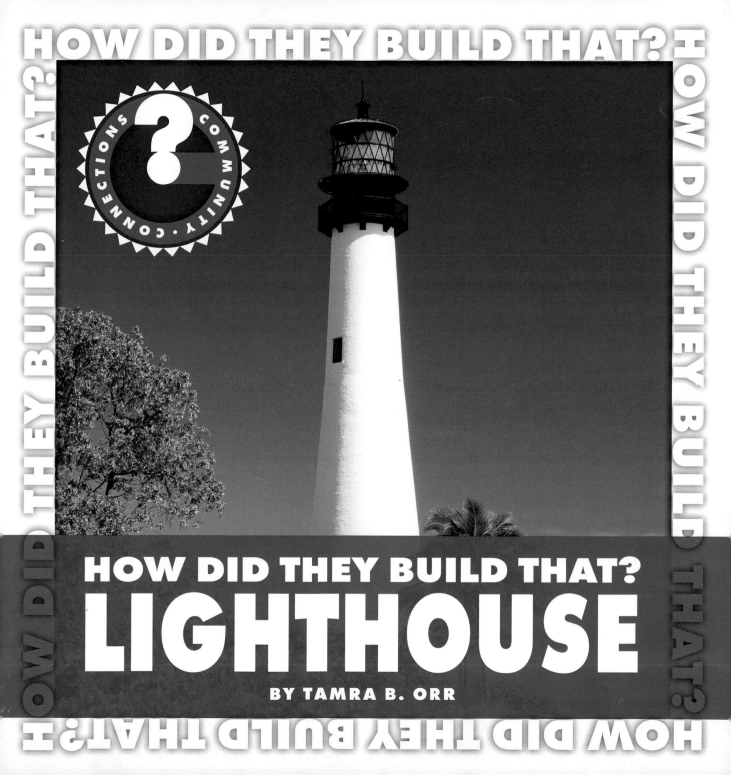

HOW DID THEY BUILD THAT?

COMMUNITY · CONNECTIONS

HOW DID THEY BUILD THAT?
LIGHTHOUSE

BY TAMRA B. ORR

CHERRY LAKE Publishing

Published in the United States of America by Cherry Lake Publishing
Ann Arbor, Michigan
www.cherrylakepublishing.com

Content Adviser: James Woodward, Owner, The Lighthouse Consultant LLC

Photo Credits: Cover and page 1, ©PHB.cz (Richard Semik)/Shutterstock, Inc.;
page 5, ©plampy/Shutterstock, Inc.; page 7, ©fstockfoto/Shutterstock, Inc.;
page 9, ©iStockphoto.com/jskiba; page 11, ©beltsazar/Shutterstock, Inc.;
page 13, ©Patricia Marks/Shutterstock, Inc.; page 15, ©iStockphoto.com/shaunl;
page 17, ©iStockphoto.com/fotique; page 19, ©iStockphoto.com/DenisTangneyJr;
page 21, ©Jason McCartney/Shutterstock, Inc.

LIBRARY OF CONGRESS CATALOGING-IN-PUBLICATION DATA
Orr, Tamra.
  How did they build that? Lighthouse/by Tamra B. Orr.
    p. cm.—(Community connections)
  Includes bibliographical references and index.
  ISBN-13: 978-1-61080-114-0 (library binding)
  ISBN-10: 1-61080-114-8 (library binding)
  1. Lighthouses—Juvenile literature. I. Title. II. Series.
  VK1013.O77 2011
  387.1'55—dc22   2011000166

Cherry Lake Publishing would like to acknowledge the
work of The Partnership for 21st Century Skills. Please
visit www.21stcenturyskills.org for more information.

Printed in the United States of America
Corporate Graphics Inc.
July 2011
CLFA09

LIGHTHOUSE

CONTENTS

FINDING YOUR WAY HOME

Imagine being lost at sea. The only thing you can see is water on every side of your boat. You ride the waves up and down. Water splashes over the edge of the boat. You are cold and wet. You are scared. Which way is land?

The sea can be a dangerous place.

Wait! What was that shining in the dark night? Was it a bright light?

You watch carefully. The light comes around again. It's a lighthouse!

You sigh with relief. Now you know how to find land. The lighthouse will guide you to safety.

A shining lighthouse is a welcome sight for sailors.

Look up Pharos of Alexandria the next time you are online or at a library. It was the first lighthouse ever built. An earthquake destroyed it in the 14th century. Today, people who study lighthouses are called **pharologists**.

Lighthouses have saved many lives since they were invented. They help guide sailors to land. They also help warn ships of rocks and other dangers.

For centuries, lighthouses worked like the traffic lights of the sea. They told people out on the water where to go and where not to go.

Many lighthouses were built to help keep ships from crashing into dangerous rocks.

NIGHT LIGHTS

All lighthouses have a bright light called a **beacon** at the top. The beacon **rotates** and shines through big windows.

Lighthouses have rooms for storing supplies and tools. Each lighthouse also has a **watch room**. That is where a **lighthouse keeper** used to sit at night. Tall spiral staircases inside lighthouses let people climb to the top.

Motors rotate the beacon.

Early lighthouses were made out of whatever people could find in the area. Some lighthouses were made of stone and brick. Others were built with wood or iron.

Newer lighthouses are built with concrete and steel. These materials are inexpensive and easy to find. They can also be formed into interesting shapes.

Lighthouses are built from strong materials so they won't be destroyed by storms or waves.

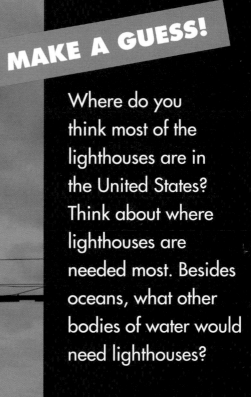

MAKE A GUESS!

Where do you think most of the lighthouses are in the United States? Think about where lighthouses are needed most. Besides oceans, what other bodies of water would need lighthouses?

13

ALL SHAPES AND SIZES

There are many different kinds of lighthouses. Some are round and very tall. Others are **octagonal**. This means they have eight flat sides. Lighthouses on cliffs or mountains are usually short and wide. That is because they are already up high.

Some lighthouses have flat sides.

Many older lighthouses are attached to small houses. These houses are where the lighthouse keepers lived. Lighthouse keepers were in charge of making sure that beacons kept shining.

Today, lighthouses no longer need keepers. Instead, they are empty and **automated**. Computers help keep beacons shining.

Sometimes a lighthouse keeper lived in a small house attached to a lighthouse.

There wasn't any electricity when the first lighthouses were built. How do you think lighthouse keepers made lights bright enough for sailors to see from the water?

The speed and pattern of a lighthouse's rotating lights are called its **character**. Lighthouses from different places have different characters.

Sailors have books explaining how to recognize these characters. This helps them figure out where they are when they see a lighthouse.

Sailors can recognize the character of a lighthouse beacon.

TODAY'S LIGHTHOUSES

Today, big ships often use computers instead of lighthouses. Computers can tell a ship's crew what its location is. They can also detect dangers.

Lighthouses are historic sites for touring. People visit them and remember how these bright lights saved many lives.

Old lighthouses are often popular places for people to visit when they are on vacation.

Next time you see a
lighthouse, look at the
patterns painted on it.
What shapes do
you see?

GLOSSARY

automated (AW-tuh-may-tid) done automatically, usually by a computer or other machine

beacon (BEE-kuhn) the bright light at the top of a lighthouse

character (KA-rik-tur) pattern of lights used by a lighthouse

lighthouse keeper (LITE-hauss KEE-pur) person in charge of running and maintaining a lighthouse

octagonal (ok-TAG-uh-nuhl) eight-sided

pharologists (fare-OL-uh-jists) people who study lighthouses

rotates (ROH-tates) spins

watch room (WAHCH ROOM) a room where the lighthouse keeper kept watch at night

FIND OUT MORE

BOOKS

Clifford, Mary Louise. *Mind the Light, Katie: The History of Thirty-Three Female Lighthouse Keepers.* Alexandria, VA: Cypress Communications, 2006.

Gauch, Sarah. *Voyage to the Pharos.* New York: Viking Juvenile, 2009.

House, Katherine. *Lighthouses for Kids: History, Science, and Lore with 21 Activities.* Chicago: Chicago Review Press, 2008.

WEB SITES

PBS: Legendary Lighthouses
www.pbs.org/legendarylighthouses/
Check out pictures and histories of many U.S. lighthouses.

Science, Optics & You: How Does It Work? Lighthouses
micro.magnet.fsu.edu/optics/activities/teachers/lighthouses.html
Learn more about how people built different kinds of lighthouses.

INDEX

ABOUT THE AUTHOR

Tamra Orr is the author of more than 250 books for readers of all ages. She, her husband, and four children live in the Pacific Northwest. They have toured half a dozen lighthouses throughout Oregon and California so far!